OVERCOMING THE STORMS OF LIFE

YOU DON'T NEED TO BE A FAITH EVACUEE

KEITH HERSHEY

Press ~ Promotions ~ Productions

Unless otherwise indicated, all Scripture quotations are taken from the New King James Version of the Bible.

Overcoming the Storms of Life
ISBN 0-940487-19-5
Copyright ©2008 Keith Hershey
Cover Design: Carlo Krouzian
P.O. Box 951060, Mission Hills, CA 91395
All rights reserved
Manufactured in the United States of America

OVERCOMING THE STORMS OF LIFE

YOU DON'T NEED TO BE A FAITH EVACUEE

KEITH HERSHEY

CONTENTS

CHAPTER ONE

How Do Personal Storms Start?

"And there arose a great storm of wind"(Mark 4:37)

Every storm starts with depression.

Have you ever watched a meteorologist give a weather report during the season when hurricanes are predicted to crash into Florida and along the Gulf Coast? They stand in front of their big map and say, "Now down here in the Atlantic, off the coast of Florida, there's a depression. It's called a *low- pressure* system." Every storm starts with depression.

Depression has turbulence in it. The low pressure has turbulence. If the low pressure with a natural storm doesn't meet high pressure, it will begin to move. It's attracted to land and moves toward land. As it moves in that direction it picks up power and moves across various states and communities and wreaks havoc. However, if low pressure meets high pressure, the high pressure *always trumps the* low pressure and *it stops the storm!*

This correlates to our lives. Life's lows are always depressing. In life, every storm, every spiritual storm or natural storm or relational storm, starts with depression. Every storm that visits me *always starts with depression*! It's a low time in life. You and I are not exempt from life's lows. That's why we must counter them by taking every pressure point and problem into God's presence and let the ***Most High*** trump life's lows. That's the way to stop our storms.

I used to think that when you gave your life to Jesus and were born again, things would go smoothly from then on. But life's just not that way. Jesus told us in Matthew 5:45 that our Father sends rain upon the just and the unjust alike. You are not exempt from life's load just because you're a follower of Jesus Christ. You're still going to find pressure, turbulence and storms in your life that try to make you move out of a faith position.

The devil doesn't mind if you believe in God, as long as you can't activate God's promises. It's only faith that takes the promises and brings them into the natural realm. So, the devil doesn't mind "unbelieving" believers, so to speak. Our culture is full of "unbelieving believers;" people who have departed from faith. When you depart from faith, from trusting, you'll begin to live like you are losing. You'll give heed to every other voice, but the voice of the Lord. And when that happens, you lose strength.

I want to teach you how to stay strong in the storms of life, so you won't become a *faith evacuee.* We have all heard the term evacuee, used frequently on the news. It's a term used to describe what happens to thousands of people in the wake of hurricanes or other devastating tragedies in America and around the world.

Once I was in the Gulf States some time after hurricanes Katrina and Rita occurred. I was visiting pastor friends in Louisiana and Mississippi. When the storms came through they did massive damage to some of my friends' churches. One of these pastor friends told us the damage to his church was over two million dollars. It tore the roof off, and all of the sound system and TV equipment were destroyed. Another pastor told me the hurricane hadn't done much damage to the church building, but the people had left. They became evacuees. They went to places like Colorado, California, Illinois, and New York. Over a year later they had not come back. They departed from the place where they were planted and became evacuees.

That's what can happen spiritually speaking, as a result of the pressures and storms of life. Because of all the voices crying out against God's Word, we begin to give heed to them and eventually we throw up our hands and scream and run. There are times in my life that I'd like to take a prolonged sabbatical until Jesus comes. When life is difficult, it seems the quickest way to deliver myself from trouble and problems is to run away. Life is often full of hardship and pain and difficult circumstances. So you've got to know where God has planted you and how to be positioned in faith so His blessings can flow through you.

Don't allow yourself to depart from that place of usefulness and power. Don't allow depression, and fear, worry and anxiety to take residence in you. Learn how to quench the turbulence and stop the storm. The same atmospheric depression principles described by the meteorologists are also true in our lives. These daily highs and lows, these low-pressure areas and times *could* cause spiritual depression. However, we need not be overcome by these spiritual atmospheric conditions. We need not be forced to move from, or to evacuate our spiritual position of faith. We can remain firm and steadfast and overcome them.

What are these low-pressure, *storm starter* areas we all face, that could result in spiritual depression? Or evacuation? And, what can we do to about them?

We know that faith comes by hearing and hearing by the word of God. (Romans 10:17) You can't depart from something unless you have something. So you can't depart from faith unless you have it already. You gain faith by hearing faith words and you lose faith by hearing fear words, by taking heed to the wrong voices. It's not that you live in the denial of what's happening naturally; you just bring a higher truth to the facts you see. The Truth of God's Word takes us to a different environmental realm than what we experience in the world. You're not denying the circumstance; you just say you're going to the Higher Power, the high pressure to nullify the effects of the low pressure or the depression in life.

You and I as believers in the faith, must position ourselves to take a spiritual truth and make it fruitful. Jesus talked about that. The fruitful element can have different intensities,

30, 60, or 100 fold. I tell people that if you don't have any joy, if you're fully depressed, start with something even if it's only a quarter of a smile. You can't get to full strength in the joy of the Lord or the peace of God and His provision in everything, unless you start some place. You need to bring the spiritual reality into the natural realm.

In Mark 4:35, the Bible tells us that on the same day the faith preacher preached the faith message, the disciples heard it. So on that day the disciples had faith because they heard the message. Faith comes by hearing. The same evening, Jesus said, "Let us cross over to the other side." Now, see what happens. A great wind storm arose; turbulence, life lows, trouble, depression. Every time you choose to believe a promise of God you're going to attract trouble; because, Satan will come immediately to try to steal it. The devil wants to put life lows or circumstances in your life to make you think that you're never going to get where Jesus said you're going.

Verse 37: "The wind storm arose and the waves beat into the boat so it was already filling." If you're in a boat that's filling and you're in the middle of the sea, it's not looking good. So these disciples who had heard – and believed – a faith message earlier that day, had a decision to make. Either take Jesus' word as final authority or just take the voices of everything else they heard and saw. What did they do?

They began to act like they were losing.

They departed from faith. And anytime you depart from

faith you'll begin to live like you're losing. You'll think you're going down. You think you're going to be the first one fired, that nothing good will every happen to you, you'll never get a good education. You'll think this, that and the other. Instead of reacting like this, we need to respond the way Jesus did with the pressures in His life.

Jesus never yielded to a natural circumstance that countered what He had decreed. He did not give heed to it. He spoke to the storm and to the sea, He said, "Peace be still." *The Word that you believe* equips you with authority to take you where you want to go.

If you don't believe a promise you won't say anything. But if you believe a promise for your healing, for your peace, for your marriage, for your church, for your community, for your world, *then you'll say something against the trouble.* You'll trouble your trouble with a Higher Authority, the Word of God. You've got to decree a thing. You've got to speak to the trouble with authority. Jesus spoke to the storm, He spoke to the sea and then look what the Bible says, "The wind ceased."

The high pressure always trumps the low pressure.

Jesus spoke and, "The storm ceased and there was a great calm." Jesus became a *storm stopper.* How do you stay strong in the storms of life? You've got to be a *storm stopper.* Look at verse 40, "But Jesus said to them, why are you so fearful. How is it that you have no faith?" Remember, faith comes by hearing and hearing by the Word of God. Jesus, the greatest faith teacher of all, had just preached the greatest faith message of all times. So how can these guys have no faith on the very day they heard Jesus' faith message? Faith comes and faith goes. Life creates leaking opportunities.

That is why you need to stay refilled with a believing heart, because every day you're going to be challenged. Every day your mind is going to be bombarded with turbulence in your world. It may be at your work or at your home, in your community, or in your church. Then you must make the decision; I'm not going to yield to depression.

What was the difference between Jesus and the disciples? They were all in the same storm, they felt the same wind, and they saw the same waves beat in and fill the boat. *The difference is that although Jesus was in the storm He did not allow the storm in Him.*

In life there are going to be troubles. I don't deny the negative circumstances. I know they are there. But I don't let them in my heart. The Bible teaches in Proverbs chapter 4 that you and I have to guard our hearts with all diligence, for out of our hearts flow the issues of life. So *you can be in trouble without trouble being in you.* Jesus was in the storm without the storm being in Him.

Whereas the disciples, who were also in the storm, allowed the storm to be in them. This is obvious because they cried out for fear. Their words came out of the abundance of their heart. What you say tells where you are. This is an amazing principle and I know from personal experience that it always shows me what is truly in my heart.

When the disciples asked Jesus about the signs of His coming, He indicated there would not only be natural disasters and challenges, but also enormous spiritual pressures in the earth. When Paul wrote to Timothy, he let him know that the Holy Spirit is speaking very clearly, clarifying that in the latter times, because of pressure, because of what people are giving heed to, because of listening to the wrong voices, people will give heed to deceiving spirits, or doctrines of demons (I Timothy 4:1).

The Scripture says, because of these pressures, people would depart from the faith. I call this becoming faith evacuees; departing from faith. Faith in God is the only place where God's Word can work with consistency in your life. Our faith in God is a personal relationship. It's not something we can borrow from a mother or a father or a spouse. We need a personal, living faith. That way, when the storms of life visit us we don't become a faith evacuee. We don't depart from faith.

Sometimes in our lives, we're so battered by storms and bruised by circumstances we don't recognize that we've departed from faith. We still have a religious identity about things we supposedly believe. But we don't have an active, vibrant living, nurturing faith to stabilize us in life's storms. And that stabilizer is the Holy Spirit whom Jesus has sent to be our Helper in all things.

We have an example of the Holy Spirit's power in lives in Acts, chapter 19. This chapter is about Paul the Apostle's visit to Ephesus. He talked to believers there and asked them if they'd received the Holy Spirit when they believed. When Paul heard they had not received the Holy Spirit, Paul laid his hands on the believers and the Holy Spirit came upon them and equipped them supernaturally. The Bible says they spoke with tongues and they prophesied. (Acts 19:6)

Paul stayed with the folks in Ephesus about two years, where he taught the Word and reasoned with them and they heard the Word (Verse 10). Look what happened next in verses 11,12. "Now God worked unusual miracles by the hands of Paul, so that even handkerchiefs or aprons were brought from his body to the sick, and the diseases left them and the evil spirits went out of them." Talk about a *storm stopper*!

Pieces of cloth that touched Paul carried the Holy Spirit's anointing power so that diseases left people and evil spirits went out of them. That *storm stopping* anointing was transferable, but not transferable for just anyone's use.

Verse 13 continues by saying, "Then some of the itinerant Jewish exorcists *took it upon themselves* to call upon the name of the Lord Jesus Christ." Then as now, there are a lot of people who believe they believe in the Lord, but really don't. They don't have a personal faith. They don't understand that sometime ago they have departed from faith, and are really trusting in other things.

These itinerant Jewish exorcists simply "borrowed" the name of Jesus Christ. They weren't really living for Jesus. They just wanted to utilize His name to "perform exorcisms in the name of Jesus" whom Paul preached.

Among these were the seven sons of Sceva, a Jewish

chief priest, who tried to utilize the name of Jesus and decree authority on storms of life that had come against people. But, since they had no genuine authority, their attempts backfired. "Then the man in whom the evil spirit was, leaped on them, overpowered them, and prevailed against them, so that they fled out of that house naked and wounded" (verse 16).

"This became known both to all Jews and Greeks dwelling in Ephesus, and fear fell on them all, and the name of the Lord Jesus was magnified. And many who had believed came confessing and telling of their deeds" (verses 17-18).

So the seven sons of Sceva really got themselves into trouble by attempting to use religious, spiritual tools they weren't equipped by God to operate. The resulting demonic storm activity devastated them, because they didn't know they were functioning outside the faith of God. They mistakenly tried to use God's special spiritual equipment thinking that it would work *just because they spoke it*.

But, if we are to witness victorious manifestations of miracles, we must truly believe in the name of the Lord Jesus and embrace God's Word, so that we don't "quench the Holy Spirit" and hinder Him in the work Jesus has sent Him to do.

Verse 18 in that same chapter of Acts indicates that, "many *had* believed." In other words, *it was past tense*. They had believed some time previously. But now, they "came confessing and telling their deeds," because they saw how seven sons of a priest, had a storm tearing their lives apart because they tried to do the Holy Spirit's job without Him. The Holy Spirit manifests Himself through God's Words of faith. "For the Word of God is living and powerful…" (Hebrews 4:12).

So we need to take a daily inventory of our faith life, our faith words. And if things aren't right, if we're paying more attention to the fear storm signs than to God's faith Words, then we are missing the mark, we are sinning and need God's forgiveness. That's what is so beautifully comforting about 1 John 1:9, "If we confess our sins, he (Jesus) is faithful and just to forgive us of our sins and to cleanse us from all unrighteousness."

So if you've become a faith evacuee, you can immediately re-establish yourself by strengthening yourself in God's Word and your faith will grow and you will become strong again. Then the power of Jesus' name and life will be manifested in through your faith.

As we saw in Acts 19, people who try to use God's name and His Word without His power find that the Word of God is a two-edged sword. For operating in God's power takes a genuine, authentic spiritual relationship that comes from being right with God. So friend, don't wait, take inventory today. And if your life is leaking faith, confess your sin, ask the Lord Jesus to cleanse you. And, according to I John 1:9, He will.

Remember Paul's admonition to Timothy, "The Spirit spoke expressly that in the latter times some will depart from faith" (I Timothy 4:1). You don't want to be one of those faith evacuees. You don't want to depart from faith. You don't want to be powerless. You want the victorious power of the Holy Spirit Jesus has provided to always be active and operating strong in your life.

So let's remember to *watch what we say,* because words are our faith barometer. Jesus told us so in Matthew 12:34, "Out of the abundance of your heart your mouth speaks." In other words, Jesus said that what you are full of is released in words. When you speak, what's in your heart is downloaded, and has the authority of your words.

Jesus lived that way. He continually said, "I only speak the things I hear my Father speak." (John 14:10) In other words, Jesus did not become a faith evacuee when He was tempted or overwhelmed by a life storm.

Jesus received a lot of scorn, a lot of pressure, a lot of potentially hurtful scenarios in His life and ministry that could have been absolutely overwhelming. When He had crowds of people trying to kill Him, when people planned His demise, "Jesus passed through the crowds" (Luke 4:30), because His faith preserved Him. Jesus made statements like, "Satan has nothing in Me" (John 14:30). He came to a place where the storm couldn't take Him out.

Jesus laid down His life willingly. He did it in the timing of the Father and not before. He did it the right way. He lived according to the plans and purposes of the Father. He knew what He was here for, and He knew He was going to accomplish what God had called Him to do. Jesus always spoke the words of His Father.

We have to live by His example; by always speaking what the Father, or the Word of God, says about our lives. That's why renewing our minds with the Word of God

(Rom. 12:2), is so significant, so powerful, and so important. God's Word equips us with faith. Faith comes by hearing and hearing by the Word of God. (Romans 10:17)

We need to be well equipped by hearing the Word of God and continually speaking it, if we want to live as a storm stopper and not a faith evacuee.

CHAPTER TWO

Don't Become a Faith Evacuee

*" . . . and the waves beat into the ship,
so that it was now full" (Mark 4:37).*

*Don't live like a loser, when you can
live like a winner.*

Difficulties in life can be compared to storms, or even to boxing matches. In fact, the strategy or our Enemy is much like the strategy in a boxing match. The opponent wants to *knock the wind out of you,* or knock you in the head. But, ultimately, he wants to take you down. The Apostle Paul used a metaphor about boxing in his writings. He said you don't want to just swing like you're beating the air. You want to have a systematic strategy to stay strong and get to your destination point.

The destination for a boxer is to be crowned the victor. In the spiritual arena, this means being in the presence of God. When we leave this earth arena and enter the arena of Heaven, we want to hear God's Word decreed over our lives: "Well done, good and faithful servant. Enter into the joy of the Lord."

I believe with all my heart that what God has planned for you is His best. It makes no sense to live like a loser when you can live like a winner. But we all know that in this life there are pressure points, problems, pain and discouragements. So I want to encourage you to stabilize your life against every strategy and design the Enemy may have to take you down and to take you out.

I believe Jesus has come to lift us up, to stabilize us, and to keep us strong. The Bible says, "*We can reign* in life through Jesus Christ" (Romans 5:17, emphasis mine).

When the principles of the Word of God are not just known, but *activated*, we have power. It's one thing to know truth; but it's another thing to experience truth. It's one thing to know a concept; but it's another thing when that concept becomes relevant and changes your natural realm. Think about your family for example. God didn't put you together to pull you apart. God put you together to go the distance.

It is because of His Covenant, as proclaimed in the Word of God, that you can be re-established in the faith. You don't have to flee from faith when you're under pressure, though Paul tells us that's a natural reaction to pressure. Remember his words, "Now the Spirit *expressly* says . . ." (I Timothy 4:1). In other words, Paul wants Timothy to know that the Holy Spirit is clarifying something, and He wants to make it extremely clear. He doesn't want anybody to be double minded about what is being communicated.

Paul could have said it this way, "Now the Spirit of God wants to communicate clearly." He goes on to clarify this utterly important message saying, ". . . in the latter times some will depart from faith." And today people do use the pressures of everyday life as a cause to depart from faith.

Living in this world puts much pressure on people right now. There is a lot of discouragement, a lot of overwhelming circumstances, a lot of points that cause pain. If you don't know how to stay strong in the Lord and take the hits that life brings to you, then you might go down for the count. But you will only go down for the count when you flee from or depart from the faith. Fleeing from the faith, or departing from the faith, means that the storms of life have overcome you.

In recent years there have been disasters of great magnitude all around the world. There was the tsunami that overwhelmed so much of Southeast Asia that affected three different continents; there were the earthquakes in parts of Southeast Asia that killed thousands. There were big storms that reached North America and Central America that destroyed literally hundreds of miles of property and towns and communities, killing hundreds and hundreds of people. Those natural storms are symbolic of spiritual storms that try to take you out the same way.

I am reminded of a time when I was in the Philippines with a ministry team of about thirty people. At one point, on our way back to Manila, we were met by an enormous storm, a monsoon. Our plane was the last one that was allowed to land. By the time we touched down, it was raining so hard we couldn't see. The landing field was so flooded that we had to sit on the runway until the water receded before we could get off the plane.

When they finally got us off the plane and bussed us to the terminal, we saw that the whole airport was flooded. In fact, the whole city was flooded and we couldn't go anywhere. It was practically unheard of! Sometimes life does things like that to you. It sideswipes you, like something out of the blue, and you don't know what to do.

I believe with all my heart that when the storms of life try to overwhelm you, you need to make a decision that you will not flee from your faith. You must decide that you will not become a faith evacuee. When you make this decision you will not lose your position of belief in Christ Jesus.

This is what God wants to do in each of our lives. He wants His Word to work. That's why God warns us through Paul's letter to Timothy, "Now the Spirit speaks expressly that in the latter times some will depart from the faith." This is a warning for everyone. *Some will become faith evacuees.* If you choose not to walk by faith, if you would rather walk by *sight*, you're in trouble.

The Scripture teaches that, as believers, *we **do not** walk by sight. We walk by faith.* Faith gives us a spiritual visual from God's Word that the Spirit of the Lord has got us covered, and He is going to keep us strong.

How do you stay strong in the storms of life? Because storms will come! Something invariably will go wrong. Your family will be under pressure at one time or another. Your physical body, your health, will be under attack at one time or another. Your community, your world will be challenged periodically. Jesus said that in the world, you will have tribulations, you're going to have tests, and you're going to have trials. "But, don't worry," Jesus said, "I have overcome the world" (John 16:33).

Since Jesus has overcome the trials and problems of life, we don't have to become faith evacuees and run from our trust in God. Instead, we establish our hearts in Him. We recommit our trust in Him. We understand the truth of the promises of God, and we walk in faith against the storm. The Bible teaches that you can even go *through* the fire; He'll be with you, even *through* the waters, even *through* the storms He'll be with you. (Isaiah 43:2)

Whatever storms you're facing in life, the power of the Word of God is much richer, much stronger, and you can be strong in your storms. *When the winds blow, you can stay in the spiritual flow.*

Consider the story of Nicodemus. In John's Gospel, chapter 3, Jesus meets a learned man by that name. The Bible says he was a Pharisee, a ruler of the Jews. He came to Jesus by night and said to Jesus, "Rabbi, we know that you are a teacher who came from God, and no one can do these signs that you do unless God is with him" (John 3:2).

The very first words Nicodemus spoke were in recognition of who Jesus is. Nicodemus knows that Jesus came from God, and that He was a miracle worker, and that God was with Him. Jesus replied saying, "Most assuredly I say to you,

Nicodemus, unless one is born again, he cannot see or experience the Kingdom of God" (John 3:5).

Do you know what every human heart craves? It's what Nicodemus really wanted to find out. It is the power of the Kingdom of God. Every human heart craves the God of Heaven to manifest His power in their life. Every human heart craves a personal relationship and renewal in Christ Jesus. Nicodemus wanted it sincerely. Even though he was very educated in the Scriptures, he didn't know how to experience the life of God's Kingdom.

That's true with a lot of people all over the world, in every nation, from every tribe, from every kindred. People have a desire for God, and many people know truths, or spiritual concepts about God, but it's only head knowledge, without authentic experience.

When God promises peace, that means peace is possible. *That means peace can be a possession.* When God promises joy, He means joy is possible and joy can be your possession. Do you know when God promises healing, that means healing is possible for you, and healing can be your possession. What the devil wants to do is bring a storm that will stop your faith from functioning so you become a faith evacuee. The Enemy wants to stop your faith from functioning so that it will not enter your realm as a possession, the manifestation, or the experiential reality of what you believe in faith.

When Jesus told Nicodemus, "Listen, you really have to be born again," Jesus is talking about something extremely beautiful and powerful. He is talking about a personal relationship with the God of Heaven. He's talking about this whole idea that Jesus Christ can be Lord of your life. And, so He begins to explain it, because Nicodemus asked, "How can a man be born again when he is old?"

In other words, he was asking, "How can I experience this born again life? Can a man enter a second time into his mother's womb and be born?" Jesus replied, "No, Nicodemus, that's not what I'm talking about. I'm not talking about natural birth. I'm talking about a spiritual birth."

Just as with Nicodemus, your natural problems many times can be solved spiritually. A lot of things that are troubling you in life, in your home, in your family, or in your relationships, have a spiritual solution. It starts with being born again, being born from above. You can't just believe in God. You have to invite the God of Heaven to live in you. This is what the new birth is all about.

So Jesus explained it this way in John 5:35, "Most assuredly I say unto you, unless one is born of water and the Spirit he cannot enter or experience the Kingdom of God. That which is born of the flesh is flesh, and that which is born of the Spirit is spirit. Do not marvel that I said unto you, you must be born again."

Have you been born again?

You can never stop the storms of life unless you have different authority flowing through you. In your own ability, you'll never have sufficiency. But, there is a sufficiency, ability, from God that can fix you. The key is that you must be born again. This means you yield your whole heart, your whole life to God Almighty. You must embrace and believe in His Son, in His death, burial and resurrection. And believe that Jesus Christ conquered death, hell and the grave. When you believe in Him, you receive of Him spiritually, not physically. This isn't a physical birth; this is a spiritual birth.

My wife, Heidi and I have two sons who are wonderful young men. I remember when they were both born. Wow! That was a physical birth. But I also remember the days when they gave their hearts to Jesus and decided to trust in Him. They were born again. At that moment they still looked the same physically, but spiritually there was something totally different. Now they could grow in the power of God and transform their circumstances through faith, by knowing how to be strong in their storms of life.

In His conversation with Nicodemus, Jesus spoke indirectly of storms. "The wind blows where it wishes" (John 3:8). Have you noticed that about a natural storm? Natural storms are basically just kind of turbulent, blowing wind. These natural storms start in a lull. There's kind of a low point in the atmosphere, and a storm begins to brew. Then it begins to move. It picks up steam, picks up motion and gains momentum. Then those storms run their courses. And usually, as was pointed out in the last chapter, a storm stops only when it's countered by high pressure.

And spiritually speaking, storms in your life usually start the same way: in a lull. That's why you can't allow yourself to be depressed for very long. You can't allow yourself to be down and out for the count for very long. Because, when you call it quits and evacuate, and depart from faith, you're in big time trouble. The Enemy will gain momentum like a hurricane gains momentum. And the storm becomes a whirlwind that sweeps through your world and annihilates your mind, your emotions, and your physical being.

But you can stop it.
In faith, you can be a storm stopper.

How do you fight the storm of the Enemy that comes against your life in the natural? You fight by staying in faith. Don't depart from the faith. Don't become a faith evacuee. Instead, fight that storm with all the spiritual strength and spiritual power, which is yours in Christ Jesus.

I believe that God wants us to be *storm stoppers.* He wants us to stop the effects and the influences that are trying to infiltrate our lives and bring us down. When you open your heart to Jesus, His Word, His Spirit, there's a spiritual strength that stabilizes you in the midst of a storm. God's Holy Spirit empowers you to become a *storm stopper* because God wants to keep you strong.

I believe that Jesus gave Nicodemus the secret. It's not the head knowledge that he knew that helped Nicodemus. Instead it was what the Holy Spirit brought alive in him for application in his personal life. This is what empowers a person to have great victory. Just as with Nicodemus, God wants to minister to you and He wants to do it by His Spirit.

If you're never been born again, what is holding you back? Why would you want to try to fix your life and your realm according to your ability, when you've already tried it before? It doesn't work. Why don't you allow the wind of the Spirit to come and get a hold on you, and bring you joy and peace? By believing in Christ, you allow the Spirit of God to become the greatest teacher in your life. Then, when you read and understand the Word of God, you're not trying to understand it intellectually; you're not trying to figure things out according to your natural ability. You're allowing the Holy Spirit to give you a significant solution for the storm situations in your life.

Do you know the Holy Spirit is concerned about you? Do you know God really loves you? Do you know God is not nervous about your life? Do you know that God even knows your end from the beginning?

The Bible says there is a great future for you; there is great hope for you. (Jeremiah 29:11) You don't have to be downcast, you don't have to call it quits, you don't have to be overwhelmed or worried. You can position yourself properly, and embrace the Spirit of God. You just have to be born again.

The way it happens is you open up your heart, and invite Him in. You say, "Jesus, I believe in You, because You believe in me. I love You, because You love me, Jesus. I believe You died on the cross; You were raised from the grave. Please come into my life." It's so simple and yet so powerful. The Spirit of God comes and begins to work in you. Then you can have discernment and understanding about how to move in every area of your life.

Have you tried to stand in a big storm when big winds are coming through? I remember being in Chicago, the "Windy City," during the winter, when the effects of the wind are especially noticeable. Walking down Michigan Avenue with the wind whipping all around is no easy task. And oftimes you need something solid to hold onto.

It's much the same in spiritual living. You get up every day and sense the freshness and the power of the Spirit of God as you are standing in faith. And then, this world's winds begin to blow. Don't depart from faith because of pressure. Don't evacuate but reach out for something solid, your rock. (I Corinthians 10:4) Jesus is our Rock so put your trust completely in Him and be stabilized.

When I was a boy, living in Michigan, we had big snowstorms in the winter. Out in the fields next to the roads, crews would set up snow fences. When the wind blew the snow, the snow would pile up by the fences and it wouldn't pile up on the roads. So people who understood storms and certain curves and contours of the roads strategically positioned these fences. These fences were called wind breakers.

A wind breaker, in the natural is a type of fence.

People are sometimes like these wind breaker fences. When the Spirit of God wants to move in their heart, they say, "I don't want this religious business. Oh, no, I want to be self-sufficient." And so, like the wind breaker fences that kept back the flow of the snow, these wind breaker people keep back the flow of the Spirit.

I believe there are a lot of people who want to live this victorious spiritual life with the wind of the Holy Spirit blowing as God wills through their daily life. But when the winds of unbelief begin howling, they don't know what to do. So, they become a *wind breaker of God's Holy Spirit*. They hinder and prevent the flow of God's presence and power of His Spirit in their lives.

Become a wind embracer
And you won't be a wind breaker.

Spiritually speaking, take a lesson from sailors: *Go with the flow of the Holy Spirit* and become a *wind embracer*. Did you ever watch a skilled sailor? Notice how he maneuvers his sail till it catches, or *embraces* the wind. As Ella Wheeler Wilcox wrote in her poem:

> *One ship drives east and another drives west*
> *With the selfsame winds that blow,*
> *'Tis the set of the sails*
> *And not the gales*
> *Which tells us the way to go.*

It is the set of your sail and not the winds or the sea that determines your destination. Even so, in your spiritual life, it's the set of your soul that decides whether you are a *wind breaker* or a *wind embracer.* Let the Holy Spirit work in your life right now. Embrace Him by creating an environment of faith in your life with God's Word. God wants to help you in every storm, in every doubt, in every pain, and in every trouble. His Spirit will stop every storm that comes against you if you become a *wind embracer.*

CHAPTER THREE

Jesus Was in the Storm; but the Storm Wasn't in Him.

"And he was in the hinder part of the ship, asleep . . ." (Mark 4:38).

The Apostle Paul was very specific when in I Timothy 4, he told Timothy there has to be clarity in communicating what the Holy Spirit wants to speak into each of our hearts and lives. If we restate verse 1 in today's context, Paul could have spoken this way, "The Spirit wants to say very clearly that, in the latter times, some will depart from faith, *giving heed to the storms of life."* Paul then goes on to list a variety of things that will swirl around you trying to devour you by making a tear, a leak, in your faith walk and to use wrestling terms, take you down for the count.

So, daily you choose, you make a decision. The decision is simply this: Will you operate in your authority as a *storm stopper*? You can stop the storms of life when you're in a storm, but only if you don't let the storm get in you. Don't allow fear to come in and cripple your heart. If it does, you can't express the authority that God has given you to function and operate in. Instead, stay in faith so you can annihilate every strategy of the Enemy that is coming against you.

Don't depart from faith. Don't be a faith evacuee.

Staying strong in the storms of life and being a storm stopper is what Jesus was talking about when He said, "In the world you will have tribulations. You will have storms. There will be trouble that visits you." But, He also went on to say, "Be of good cheer." He is telling us that there is an attitude we must have during pressure points.

Think of this for just a moment: The attitude most people have under pressure is despair, or discouragement, or fear, or worry, or feeling overwhelmed. And then fear grips them. They have allowed the storm to get inside them and become paralyzed by fear. Because fear and faith cannot co-exist, they depart from faith. And people then become merely religious instead of remaining in the strength of God's love, in the forceful flow of God's wind, His Spirit.

Jesus described the "wind of the Spirit"
as the Holy Spirit working in peoples' lives.
(John 3:8)

The Holy Spirit enables us to live in this life the way Jesus lived. Jesus called it "being born again." Paul said that once we've experienced this wind of God, once we put our faith in Him personally, we are transformed from the inside. God's Spirit makes us a new creation in Christ Jesus (II Corinthians 5:17), so that we can rise up with His authority. We do not need to allow ourselves to be troubled by the storm to the point that we are paralyzed and can't function in faith.

Jesus stayed strong in the storms of life. He did not allow storms to get to Him. Some people seem to think that storms come only to them. They think God has favorites. But the Bible teaches that God is no respecter of persons. (Acts 10:34)

We are living in a fallen earth, a fallen world, and storms will come. So, you have to know what to do when they come. You need to stay strong in the storms of life so you won't be blown over. It's just like when you see a natural storm coming through. You see the storm's effects. Trees are snapped and roofs are blown off. Even buildings can be blown away by big hurricane winds. But some things do survive the storms.

Spiritual storms are much the same. You can see the effects of spiritual storms of pressure and pain: marriages fall apart, people go off the deep end, people want to call it quits, they want to end their life, or jump off a bridge. They become angry and bitter, and stay that way for a decade or two. But you don't have to live life that way. As a child of God you can survive your spiritual storms.

When you're under pressure and pain, you need to run

to God, not away from Him. If you only look naturally at the trouble in your life, you might say, "Why me?" You can have all kinds of excuses. Many times people end up blaming God. They blame Him for everything bad. But, as a newborn child of God you now have authority: authority for your family, authority over your circumstances. We can rise in faith and live like Jesus lived, under the pressure points and pains of life, and accomplish what He accomplished.

Jesus taught us how to survive storms – both natural and spiritual storms.

Let's look again at how he does that. In the Gospel of Mark, chapter four, Jesus has just expounded the life of faith to His disciples. They heard His Words – and they believed. Then, on *the evening of that same day*, Jesus said to them, "Let us cross over to the other side."

Verse 37, "and a great wind storm arose…"

Turbulence, life lows, trouble, depression. Every time you choose to believe a promise, you are going to attract trouble, because Jesus told us that *Satan will come immediately* to try and steal that promise from you. *So, the devil wants to put life lows or circumstances in your life to make you think that you're never going to get where Jesus said you're going.* The Bible says, "The wind storm arose and the waves beat into the boat, so it was already filling."

If you're in a boat that's filling and you're in the middle of the sea, it's not looking good. So, these disciples who had heard a faith message had a decision to make: Either we'll take Jesus' word as final authority – or – just take the voices of everything else we hear and see.

Verse 38, *"Now Jesus was in the stern asleep on a pillow."*

Remember Jesus told us that He only spoke what the Father told Him. When Jesus said, "Let's go to the other side," it was the will of God, so He made His action to correspond with His Words. *He rested.* He rested in His faith and was able to sleep during the storm.

Jesus was in the storm, but the storm wasn't in Jesus.

But in **verse 39**, we read how the disciples exclaimed, "We're perishing!" Now Jesus was in the stern of the boat, asleep on a pillow. They awoke Him and said, "Teacher, teacher, don't You care? Don't You care we're perishing?"

Did Jesus respond to their panic and say, "My goodness, we're sinking! Dear God, what are we going to do? Grab a life vest! Jump overboard! I'll see you later!" No! Jesus never yielded to a natural circumstance that countered what He had decreed. He did not give heed to the situation. He spoke to the storm and to the sea. He quietly said, "Peace, be still."

Faith comes and faith goes. Life's full of leaks.

When the storms, the problems, come – *and they will come* – your faith, which shows in your attitude, makes all the difference. The attitude Jesus taught is to "Be of good cheer." Do you know what cheer means? *When you have good cheer, you can't be in fear."* When you're operating in the joy of the Lord and the power of God, His presence will preserve you. (Nehemiah 8:10) His cheer removes fear. The Lord wants to equip you to stay strong in the storms of life. He wants you to not only stay strong, but to be a *storm stopper*. Then the effects and influences of darkness won't hold you. Instead, you will be a *wind embracer* and move in the power of God.

With every promise that God has given, Satan has always tried to interrupt it, to keep the promise from coming to pass. But God has already made provision for the completion of each and every promise He has given. The only way for Satan's storms, his fiery darts, to hinder the fulfillment of God's promises is when we don't have faith concerning those provisions.

In Los Angeles where we have the headquarters of Mutual Faith Ministries, there are different building codes related to earthquakes. There are codes stipulating how to build buildings and how to build highways. The codes require that construction be able to withstand a certain level of earthquake activity. These different codes want to make sure that buildings are constructed in certain ways to resist the pressure of an earthquake, or a hurricane, or the winds of natural storms.

In the Gulf Coast of America, there are building codes related to hurricanes. Many times when hurricanes hit North America, some buildings are completely blown apart. Often this happens because the structures weren't built to withstand winds of 150 miles per hour. They were only built to withstand winds of 75 miles per hour. So, when the strong winds came, they were unprepared.

Similarly, you really don't know how strong the storms will be that you're going to experience. So you want to be well equipped in the Word of God, well nourished in words of faith. If you're going to be strong enough for any storm of life and not be shattered or overcome by catastrophes, you need to be properly nourished *before* the storms of life come. To do this you need to feed on the right kind of spiritual food. Jesus said that all who hunger and thirst for righteousness, *shall* be filled.

Do you have a hunger for righteousness or have you given up? Have you already departed from faith and you're not even interested in growing? Many people get discouraged in the storms of life, and blame God in the process. They think, "Oh, this religion stuff can't help me." And, it's true; *religion* will never really help. But a relationship with the *wind of the Spirit*, with the life of God, will satisfy and stabilize you in every storm of life.

If you hunger and thirst for righteousness
And feed on the spiritual food of God's Word
Then you will stay strong.

Staying strong is a commitment. Professional athletes take note of what they need to do and eat to stay physically fit and strong. They nourish themselves properly so their bodies can respond quickly under pressure to any need. If I were to be in a marathon in my present physical condition, my body wouldn't hold up under the pressure. Because I haven't prepared my body in the way professional athletes have. I haven't gone through the same physical fitness routine. I haven't eaten the all right nutrients or foods that would strengthen my muscles and bones for that type of pressure. I can handle a certain amount of physical pressure, but not what professional athletes endure. It's not possible for me to do so, because I haven't prepared myself in that way.

Spiritually speaking, you need to prepare for whatever hell may throw against you. You can do this because Jesus is on your side. God is good and His mercy endures forever. God is not anyone's problem. He is our provision. There is no reason to blame Him when a storm of life tries to take you out.

Paul instructs Timothy that he will be spiritually strong by being "nourished in words of faith and of the good doctrine which you have carefully followed. But reject profane and old wives' fables and exercise yourself toward godliness" (I Timothy 4:6-7). Paul gives Timothy insight about how not to depart from faith when the storms come. Go to God under pressure, instead of running away from God. Take the authority of His Word and let it work in your life.

When you think about physical foods and nutrition it's not just about what or how much you eat. You have to know what is good for you. Not all so-called natural food is good for you. We live in a world where most foods are pre-packaged. Many of the nutrients are cooked out of food, or burnt out, or nuked out, or microwaved and processed away. The nutritional value of the food is greatly diminished by the time you get it. This is why it's important to carefully choose foods that are nutritional and healthy before sickness, the storm, comes.

We have to make the same choices about our spiritual food. Because just as in the physical, there is a lot of junk food, likewise, there is also a lot of spiritual junk food. Just because somebody says he/she is a spiritual person, or a minister, or a reverend, doesn't mean they are truly serving God. Titles are often meaningless.

God has told us to rightly divide the word of truth. (II Timothy 2:15) So that must mean it is possible to wrongly divide it. Many people will try to sell you a bill of goods. That's why, with the help of the Holy Spirit, you have to judge all things and be discerning about what you take in, what you embrace, and what you call the will of God. There are people who will try to teach you that God is against you, wants to take you down, that He wants to take you out. But, that is not true. It is the devil that comes to steal, kill and destroy. Jesus has come to give you life abundantly. (John 10:10)

The Holy Spirit, can and will give us discernment to rightly divide if we digest, take in, the right nourishment. When the Word of God comes to you, you have to take it in faith for there to be profit or nourishment in it for you. That's what the Scripture talks about in Hebrews 4:2 when the writer says, "When the Word is preached to you, it must be mixed, taken, in faith." If you've evacuated or fled from your faith, then spiritual food won't be accessible to you.

Many people store up food in anticipation of natural

storms. Some have storm cellars or basements so that when a tornado or high wind comes through they can take shelter. Often times these shelters have stored food inside to be used when storms come. But if these people didn't have access to this food during a storm it wouldn't be of any help.

Likewise, you need spiritual food stored in your heart for when your storms come. You may not have a Bible immediately available and the stormy winds are blowing. Your spiritual food, God's provision needs to be accessible during these times of pressure. You better have prepared yourself with stored spiritual food. In every storm you will need to access God's Word, your spiritual food, that you have stored in your heart.

Successful athletes always prepare for competition *beforehand* so they're prepared for all emergencies, all storms, during competition. People living in regions subject to tornadoes or hurricanes prepare for the storms *before* storm season ever arrives. Similarly, you must prepare spiritually by studying and knowing the Word *before* spiritual storms come.

In the storms of life, you will only make right decisions if you are being nourished on words of faith. Faith-filled words are the only words that can help you. When you're overwhelmed by a storm in your life, don't let Satan deceive you into abandoning your faith. It is only faith-filled words that can help you!

If you're going to stop a storm, you have to do it in faith. When Jesus acted as a storm stopper, He used His faith. Think about the examples of Jesus' ministry in the Gospels when people had storms in their lives. Some people lost their children and they would come to Jesus in sorrow. Other people were sick and overwhelmed. There were people who had spent all their money and lost everything. But when Jesus stood beside them in their storm, He became a *storm stopper*.

He used faith-filled words. Faith has to speak. It is activated through decrees and declarations. Jesus always used faith-filled words. He was nourished in words of faith. So, when He went into a storm environment, even though He was in the storm, He didn't let the storm get in Him. He stayed in faith, rightly dividing the word of truth. He knew the will of God, and He decreed a thing. When He decreed a thing, He believed the Father would fulfill what He spoke.

In like fashion, you have to decree a thing and believe that God Almighty will fulfill what you speak, according to His promises. When you're nourished with words of faith, then you can find freedom, and victory, and joy.

The Bible says in I John 2:15, "Do not love the world or the things in the world; if anyone loves the world, the love of the Father is not in him." We have a temptation under pressure and in the storms of life to look to the world's system for our solutions. In the flesh, we sometimes like the world's ways more than God's ways. But the Bible says, "Don't love the world's ways."

Don't have a love affair with the attractions in this world. Don't let your heart be set on earthly systems or ways of living.

45

"For all that is in the world – the lust of the flesh, the lust of the eyes, and the pride of life – is not of the Father but is of the world" (I John 2:16).

I call this "spiritual junk food." This includes the lust of the flesh, the lust of the eyes, and the pride of life. During the pressure points of your life, you've got to decide whom you're going to trust and who your final authority is. A final authority is whoever or whatever eventually makes the decision. You need to make the Word of God your final authority. To avoid fleeing from the faith, you have to make the Word your standard and your focus. Then, like Jesus, when you're in a storm environment, you're not going to run from faith. Instead, you're going to operate in faith, because you are being nourished in and by faith-filled words.

How should you prepare to speak in faith? Begin by preparing for the storm in advance. You do this by having daily fellowship with the Father, pouring your heart out to Him, and taking time to worship Him. When you worship, it's refreshment, it's a renewal to your soul, your emotions, and your mind. The next thing you do is speak the promises of God that you understand from the Word. You have access to these because you are in Christ. The Bible is full of promises and it teaches that they are all "Yes and Amen." (II Corinthians 1:20) That means they are for you, so let them happen in your life. As you speak and hear the Word, your faith grows. Remember: Faith comes by hearing, and hearing by the Word of God. (Romans 10:17)

I have little passages of Scripture written out that are confessions of who I am in Christ. I read these as part of my personal or family time of devotion. As a family we read something from the Bible and then we pray together. We read promises from the Word and proclaim them to each other. We speak God's promises about our lives audibly so they are part and parcel with who we are. We decree that Jesus is Lord of our lives and we confess who we are in Christ. Our ears hear what our mouths speak. Doing this builds the spirit of faith in us.

This routine of confessing the Word is just like an athlete eating healthy and being nourished so that his body can fight off, and stop, sickness storms with great physical strength. By confessing the Word, I'm eating and being nourished with spiritual food, so that when the storms come I can stop them in the power of His spoken Word.

In Luke chapter 4 Jesus demonstrates the effectiveness of speaking the Word when under pressure from the Enemy. He had just fasted 40 days and nights. At that point, when Jesus was physically both weary and hungry, the devil came upon Him with the intention of taking Him down. But Jesus wasn't taken out – because He spoke God's Words. Jesus was spiritually nourished, made strong, by Words of faith, as He spoke them.

Jesus said, "It is written, 'Man shall not live by bread alone, but by every word of God'" (Luke 4:4). He spoke the Word. Jesus is our example to follow. In every circumstance He encountered, whether with other peoples' storms or His own, He spoke the Word. If you're not filled with words of faith, then you don't have access to strength building food, and you won't know what to speak.

What happens to a lot of people, unfortunately, is they don't know how to stop the storm, so they just cry, "Oh, God help me!" But, God has made available to you all the help you need with the authority that Jesus has given to you as a believer. You can be a *storm stopper* because you know how to decree a thing.

If sickness attacks you, and you don't know that you know…that you know…that you know, it's God's will to heal you, you're going to be overwhelmed with fear. You won't be able to move by faith. If your family is under attack, and you don't know it's God's will for you all to walk in peace, you cannot speak peace. If your finances are under attack and you don't know that you have a covenant of prosperity and provision, that God is going to provide all your needs "according to His riches in glory by Christ Jesus" (Philippians 4:19) then you will flounder unprotected in the storm.

So feed on God's Word. That's the way you become a *storm stopper.* Become "strong in the Lord in the power of His might" (Ephesians 6:10), and you can stop every storm that comes against you. Then you will know that you know…that you know…that "if God is for you and that no one can come against you" (Romans 8:31). And when you KNOW that, then you will be a mighty *storm stopper*!

CHAPTER FOUR

When Your Faith Is Working, You Will Be A Storm Stopper

"And they awoke him, and said unto him, Master, carest thou not that we perish?" (Mark 4:38).

There will be storms. And in storms, people scatter. Recall what Paul said in I Timothy 4:1, "...in the latter times some will depart from the faith." He then lists some of the pressures that will be upon people in the latter times. And, instead of trusting in God, people will trust in themselves. These are the people who will flee or "evacuate" from flowing in faith with God's Word. I call them *faith evacuees.*

If you choose to live a man-made life, according to your own ability to try and fix the challenges of your life, according to human understanding, you're going to be in trouble, big trouble! The best way, actually the only way, to stand against a storm is to be stabilized by the Holy Spirit through

God's Word and then flow by faith in God's authority. By speaking only what the Father told Him to, Jesus remained in the flow of God's Holy Spirit, even when He was in the midst of a storm.

The more things I try to fix
The more I get into a fix.

God's Word teaches us that even though there are storms in life, even though there are challenges, even though there are concerns that we may have; there are Biblical principles that can be applied to stop the storms in our lives. We can position ourselves to "cast our cares on Him, because He cares for us" (I Peter 5:7).

In the Old Testament there's a story of when the Word of the Lord came and said, "Stand still, trust in Me, and see the salvation of the Lord" (Exodus 14:13). Oftimes we try to fix everything ourselves, according to our own ingenuity, according to our plans. But, I've learned in life that the more things I try to fix what doesn't seem to be working, the more I get in a fix. We need to trust God and *let Him stop every storm.*

It is very important for all of our lives that we learn to listen to the voice of God our Father. In His Word, God frequently tells us to hear or listen so that we will follow the Father's voice. Jesus said that if we hear His voice, we can follow Him. (John 10:27) If you listen and follow, you will have a communion, an intimacy, and a relationship with God that is so personal, so strong; the Holy Spirit can empower you. God's power through His Holy Spirit in you is what enables you to stop every storm that's trying to tear you down and blow you apart.

That is why it is so crucial that you listen and follow Jesus' example during the pressure points of life. Don't yield to man-made ways of doing things. Don't flee from your faith, but rather, be an *embracer* and flow in faith. Remember that every time Jesus was in a storm, He didn't let the storm get in Him. When we study His life throughout the Gospels, we see Jesus facing both His own storms and other peoples' storms. When He found storms in peoples' lives He responded in faith. He spoke against their storm and anchored the will of God in their lives through faith declarations. Faith can function with authority when it is given a voice. You need to speak in order to decree a thing.

Let's look again at Mark, chapter 4 and in verse 35. Jesus has spoken and decreed a thing. He and the disciples who were with Him were going to go to a destination point on the other side of the lake. They all got in the boat and started across. Verse 37, "And a great windstorm arose, and the waves beat into the boat, so that it was already filling." But, Jesus was in the stern of the boat, asleep, resting and at peace. He could rest peacefully because He had spoken, He had decreed, "Let's go to the *other* side."

He knew He was in the will of His Father. He had spoken His Father's Words and He knew where He was going. So, when the storm came up, He knew it could not change what had been decreed. Jesus was in the storm but the storm was not in Him. But the disciples were not thinking about Jesus' Words, they were focusing on the circumstances, they allowed fear to come in and so, *the storm got into the disciples and they cried out for fear.* Then Jesus stood up, without any fear, and operated in faith. He spoke to the storm, "Peace, be still." And the storm ceased. *The storm wasn't in Him.*

You can live in that same fearless faith. It's called fearless faith because faith and fear are opposites and cannot occupy the same space at the same time. Fear is unable to speak to storms in authority. Only in faith can you speak to your storms. When you stand in faith and "rightly divide the Word of truth" (II Timothy 2:15) for your circumstances in life; then you can decree a thing against the forces of hell that are trying to destroy you and bring you down.

Remember God's words in Psalm 107:2 says, "Let the *redeemed* of the Lord say so." God has covered us and our faith is at hand. Galatians 3:13 tells us that we've been *redeemed* from the curse of the law. The curse is poverty, sickness, and spiritual death. So, if we're under pressure of poverty, or sickness, or spiritual death, we can fight the forces that are countering us with faith-filled words.

You've got to fight the wind of darkness with the wind of God's Spirit. Jesus told Nicodemus, "You don't know where the wind comes from, or where it's going." (John 3:8) But, life in the Spirit, the new birth is like that experience of allowing the Holy Spirit to begin to work in your life and in your midst by being an embracer:

An Embracer of God's Spirit and his Word.

Isaiah 43:1 reminds us, "Fear not, for I have redeemed you; I have called you by your name, and you are Mine." It's so very important that we understand what it means to belong to the Almighty God. For starters, it means He's got us covered.

Periodically, when my son's were very young, one or both of them would feel pressured or concerned in some way and get nervous about things of life. I would say to them, "Listen, You will have food to eat and a warm bed to sleep in. Don't worry, Daddy has got you covered." And then they would relax in faith in their Daddy's words.

Oh that we would have a childlike faith in the Words of our Heavenly Father. And when pressures arise in our lives, we would hear, really hear our Father say, "Fear not for I have redeemed you…" In other words, "Don't worry, your Father has you covered." He is our Heavenly Father and we are His kids. We need to daily remind ourselves that we are His, and, He has us covered.

He knows your end from your beginning. He knows what you're going through. He knows the storm that's trying to infiltrate your realm. But, He's not nervous, so why should you be nervous? He has already told you, "I have called you by name, you are Mine." (Isaiah 43:1)

You're not just going to go to it
You're going to go through it.

In the next verse, God gives a decree concerning us, "When you pass *through* the water I will be with you." Notice that you are going to pass *through* the water. You're going to go *through*…you're not just going *to* it, you're not just going to end up in it…you're going *through* it.

God's promise gets even better. "When you pass through the water," God says, "I will be with you. And through the rivers, they shall not overflow you. When you walk through the fire, you shall not be burned, nor shall the flames scorch you. For I Am the Lord your God, the Holy One of Israel, your Savior." (Isaiah 43:2-3) Isn't that wonderful! God is our Redeemer and the Savior of each and every one of us who choose to believe. If you know, that you know, that you know this promise, you won't flee from faith when you're under pressure.

Let's consider how this passage in Isaiah relates to I Timothy, chapter 4. We've been looking at how can we avoid becoming one of those who depart from faith, giving heed to the storms of life? So in order to keep your heart fixed and trusting in the Lord, don't allow the world's system to distract you. Don't allow man-made, secular opinions to influence you. Know that you are the redeemed of the Lord and begin to speak it out loud. Rejoice, knowing that when you're in a storm situation, you're not going to be overcome by it, because God is with you and *you are going through.*

Recognize The Signs of a Faith Evacuee.

"And he said unto them, Why are you so fearful? How is it that you have no faith?" (Mark 4:40).

Adam and Eve lived in faith and spoke in faith until that fateful day in the Garden of Eden, when Adam and Eve "sold out" to "the god of this world" (II Corinthians 4:4), and put all of mankind under the control of darkness. Which means we all live in a fallen world. It isn't perfect any more. On that day, the power and authority God gave to Adam (and all of mankind) was usurped by Satan. Sin came into the world and has been in control ever since. It's time for you and me to take back the authority over the powers of darkness. And we can do it through the power we now have in Christ Jesus.

When Jesus came to the earth He restored us to fellowship with the Father. And now, once again, we have access to Heaven from the earth. The will of God can be established in this earth, through believing people who know how to flow in the authority and power of Jesus' name.

How can you recognize if you've departed from faith and become a faith evacuee?

Faith evacuees are known by the words they speak.

I can tell when I'm in danger of becoming a faith evacuee based on what I say. Actions usually follow words. Sometimes we can control our actions for a while and deceive others. We may go to a church service and smile and say, "Hallelujah," clap our hands, sing a song – appear to worship the Lord – and pray. But if this is done out of religious tradition, duty, and deceit, after a time, our actions will follow what's in our heart and mouth and we will be known for what we are: a faith evacuee.

There are signs you can see (and hear) in yourself that will help you to know if you have departed from the faith and become a faith evacuee. By becoming aware of this, you can position yourself firmly in your faith.

To begin with, we must measure the words we speak. Faith speaks. And, if you've departed from faith, you won't speak faith-filled words. A believing heart speaks faith. A believing heart decrees things. You can tell if you believe or if you doubt – whether you are faith-filled, or fear-filled – strictly by what you say.

If you *speak the Word of God during a storm*, when natural circumstances attempt to overwhelm or violate what you know is in God's Word, then you are speaking in faith. When you hear yourself speak faith-filled words, it reminds you that you have not departed from faith.

No one else really knows what we say more than ourselves. And I know that if I don't guard my heart, I can buy into negative self-talk. Negative self-talk is when you are extremely hard on yourself, when you demean yourself and minimize your circumstances and environment, based on what you see.

Unfortunately, when storms happen in life, whether natural or spiritual, people tend toward negative self-talk, by asking questions like, "Why? Why God? Why me?" You may not immediately know or understand the reason for a storm; but whatever the reason, all storms will increase in intensity with negative talk and self-doubt. The enemy of your soul is present in such words, because he is the thief that has come to "steal, kill and destroy" you (John 10:10).

Negative self-talk is a poison that paralyzes people because it makes them depart from faith, and they begin to trust in their own self-sufficiency.

This is the place where Jesus impacts our lives. He said, "All power is given unto Me" (Matthew 28:18), then He gives us the power we need, "over all the power of the enemy" (Luke 10:19). With that power at our disposal, Jesus commands us to go into the whole world and exercise that power for others. (Matthew 28:19)

There's a reason why Jesus has given such power and authority to us. It's for the preservation of people on our planet.

You and I have potential access to all of God's power in our lives right now. You don't have to be overwhelmed by the storms of life. You don't have to be blown apart or have your whole world come apart during times of storm and stress.

Those storms are the work of the devil, he is trying to hinder you. To stop you from getting to the place that God has called you to go. God has a destination for you – a place of service where He can use you. (Jeremiah 29:11) And, as you go – in His name – His presence and power are always available if we continually abide under the shadow of the Almighty. That's the place where He can align our hearts, and we can boldly go in faith to do what God wants us to do.

Saying the words of that wonderful 91st Psalm, you can put yourself in agreement with God's Words. "You are our refuge. You are our fortress. You are our God. You are our strength. I can trust in you."

You don't have to evacuate from a life of faith. Instead, you can activate your faith in God to stop every disaster that tries to tear you world apart, or your family, or your home, or your finances, or your health. You can stop every storm of life if you:

Become a wind embracer instead of a wind breaker.

We are filled with the wind of God when we are born again. As new creations in Christ Jesus, we walk in His strength when we allow the winds of the Spirit to blow in us – without hindrance – giving us His presence and power, the assurance that God Himself is living in us.

You can fight the natural strategies of hell with spiritual strategies from Heaven when the Spirit of God comes in you. You can embrace the winds of the Spirit of God and be led by that Holy Spirit. (Romans 8:14) Then you will be given insight, understanding, and revelation to do what He wants you to do. (Proverbs 4:7)

Remember how Jesus and His disciples responded differently to the same terrible storm that came to them, as recorded in the Gospel of Mark, chapter 4.

Circumstances can be puzzling and overwhelming in the natural – with your kids, in your family, or your physical body. Even like the situation that was developing in the boat for Jesus and His disciples. Even as their boat was filling with water, everything in your life may be filling with negatives and seems to be going wrong.

As bad as the situation looked to the disciples, it wasn't bothering the Master at all. "He was in the stern, asleep on a pillow" (verse 38). A point to remember is this: He was in the storm, but *the storm was not in Him*.

It is so very important to understand this concept of not fleeing from your faith. Don't become a faith evacuee. Instead, stay strong. ***Know*** in whom your have believed, and ***be persuaded*** that He is able to ***keep and guard, and protect that which*** He has given to you, even until that great day when He comes again! (I Timothy 1:12)

I find it interesting that the disciples asked Jesus, "Teacher do you not care that we're perishing?" Even people who seem strong in faith sometimes become faith evacuees. Many people who love God still get nervous about everything. They wring their hands in worry. They buy into despair. They *talk about all the overwhelming problems,* and about how everything is going to go wrong.

Faith evacuees want you to join them.

Don't join them. Say to yourself, "I refuse to fear. I'm going to trust I'm *not* going to stay with the storm winds of circumstances. God, I'm going to stay with the winds of the Spirit of God. I'm going to stay in the power and the presence of

God, and let God be my provision.

When Jesus' disciples asked Jesus if He cared about their well-being, He did what He always does: He showed them how to use His authority and power. "He arose and rebuked the wind and said to the sea, 'Peace, be still!' and the wind ceased and there was a great calm."

Jesus was a storm stopper. Jesus was led by the Spirit of God in such a way that He stopped the storms of life that raged around Him. The disciples, instead, to whom Jesus had given the same authority and power, and the same assignment from the heart of God, became faith evacuees. They could have risen up in faith, but instead, they fled from their faith. They failed to function in their faith with a declaration.

How does faith function? *It speaks.* Jesus spoke to the storm. He spoke to trouble. Most of the time, when we have trouble, *instead of speaking **to** the storm,* we speak **about** *the storm* until it becomes so magnified in our mind that we become nervous and fearful.

We think and speak about it at night and are unable to sleep. We become overwhelmed with worry and torment. What we should do is fight the storm with the spiritual power of faith that's available, by speaking in faith. Faith functions when we speak what God speaks.

That's what Jesus always did. He spoke to the storm and rebuked it. Think about that. He simply spoke to the storm and commanded it to cease. And the storm did just that: it ceased! Let's say, for example that your life is filled with uncertainties, such as in your home or in your marriage. These may come because of pressures and frustrations, or lack of communication and anger, or whatever the situation may be. What are you going to do about it?

You need to find a quiet place in your heart, where you can be at peace, and put your trust in God. Speak to Him, "Father, I believe You are going to preserve my home and family." Then – instead of speaking *about* the trouble – speak *to* the trouble as Jesus spoke to the storm. In the Name of Jesus, speak to the forces of hell that are behind the storms in your life, and command them to depart from your life.

Maybe your storm is a physical sickness or problem, or some other attack of the enemy. What you need to do for your faith to function is *speak to it.* Speak *to* the sickness. Speak *to* the headache. Speak *to* the pain in the Name of Jesus.

Faith functions when you give it your voice and decree a thing. Faith produces a strong authority when you speak God's Word from your heart. God's Word declares, "By His stripes *we are* healed" (Isaiah 53:5). You can live your life without fleeing from faith, by being strong in faith, "giving glory to God" (Romans 4:20).

This shows us how Jesus became a storm stopper.

He spoke to the storm. He rebuked the sea and commanded, "Peace! Be still."

Why don't you do the same? Say "Peace! Be still!" over the trouble that's in your children. Speak *to* those troubles, instead of magnifying the challenges, rebellion and bad decisions by speaking *about* them. Believe God for your children. Love them with God's love. Don't let the storm drive you out of a faith-focus and into the natural realm.

Your problems aren't going to be fixed with natural solutions. They can only be fixed when you come to the place where God's Word is preeminent and brings lasting, spiritual solutions.

In these latter days men will depart from the faith because of pressures and challenges. (I Timothy 4).

In Mark 4:40 Jesus asked His disciples, "Why are you so fearful? How is it that you have no faith?" He had a good reason for the question. He had just demonstrated God's power and authority by speaking to the storm; the same power and authority God had made available to them, and now they were faltering and fearful.

Keep in your mind that everything in the Kingdom of God functions on the principle that "Faith comes by hearing and hearing by the Word of God" (Romans 10:17). Though the disciples had been thoroughly exposed to this principle, when they were faced by the natural pressures in their real world, their faith became paralyzed, fear came in and they departed from faith.

If you find yourself crippled by fear; if fear-thinking dominants your mind, you're in trouble. What can you do? You must fight fear with faith words. Faith works and becomes an active force when faith words are spoken. Jesus repeatedly demonstrated this: In trying circumstances, He displaced fear with faith.

That's the answer. Under the pressure of a storm, stop the storm through faith. As you learn to flow in the Holy Spirit, He teaches you how to stay faithful…full of faith. He will teach you the words to use in talking to others.

I meet many wonderful, precious people in my ministry. Some are under crushing pressures. In times of fellowship with these people, often for just a short time, God is teaching me how to be a storm stopper for them, and to teach them how to do the same. When I am talking to people one-on-one, or to a large audience, I am learning how to pray and how to speak with them against their storms. I don't take on their worries. I try to understand their struggles, without embracing them.

I don't allow the storms swirling around my life to get into me and I don't allow the storms swirling around others to get into me.

In life we have to know how to deal with turbulence. I fly a lot, and when we hit turbulence, I don't like it. When the plane begins to bounce around and drop and lift and bounce and move. I don't like it, because I'm in the air and I want the plane to get to its destination. So what I do is pray, because I believe I'm on an assignment from the Father. The Spirit of God has opened an opportunity and assigned my heart with a message to share, so I believe I have His authority to speak to the turbulence.

I remember one time I was on a little prop plane flying in the Gulf States. The plane was jam packed with passengers. It was a little twin-engine plane, and we hit a storm. The plane didn't have enough power to get above the storm and it wasn't quick enough to get around it. So we had to fly through this massive storm. The plane vibrated and shook and lifted and a few times it dropped hundreds of feet at once. People were crying out. They were sick. They had their little bags out and people who didn't know God were looking for Him. People were virtually paralyzed with fear.

People were crying all over the plane and so the stewardess at the front started rolling bottles of wine down the aisle. People would grab them, open them, and just start guzzling. The world's system needs to be intoxicated or medicated to deal with fear. They want to be numb. They think if they're numb the pain won't hurt. But instead, it just prolongs and deepens it.

As others panicked in fear, I chose to read my Bible, speak the Word, and take authority. Even so, I was so nervous I couldn't pray in English anymore. I started praying in the Spirit. But I did not give into fear. I did not evacuate my faith.

You can be bold like that when you're dealing with the turbulence of your life. It's better to give your storm to God because His high power will always stop the enemy's lower power. Give your ways to God and refuse to fear or else fear will paralyze you.

When I'm in the storm, I don't want that storm to paralyze me. I don't want to flee from my faith and stand in fear, because then I'll go down. I don't want to go down for the count, do you? I don't want my ship to sink, do you? I don't want my family to fail, do you?

Jesus handled the pressure of multiple storms all through His life. And He did it with dignity, strength and authority. Even when Judas came with all the soldiers, to betray Him with a kiss, Jesus didn't depart from faith. Whereas Peter, in the midst of the same storm at Gethsemane, once again looked at the natural circumstances. He forgot all about the Words of Jesus and he departed from faith. Peter used his natural understanding, drew his sword and sliced off the ear of a servant of the high priest.

Even at that moment Jesus remained unperturbed. "Hey, Peter, this isn't the time, that's not My Father's way. He has a better plan . . ." And Jesus calmly restored the man's ear. Even under the unimaginable pressure of that hour, in the midst of His own storm, Jesus stopped another man's storm. Jesus was a blessing to the enemies who had come to take Him down.

Jesus understood something they could never know. They could not take Him down, not ever, because He willingly laid down His life – for us, for you and for me.

Jesus had already settled His destination with His Father. They were in perfect agreement. The final destination was to be the Cross; for the salvation of all of us who chose to believe in

Him. A Plan set in motion before the world began – for us to do His will, and to have access to the Father.

Even knowing what was to happen to Him – how He would be scourged, and forced to carry His own Cross, and to hang on that Cross, and to die – didn't cause Jesus to lose faith. Because He knew His destiny and His final destination. That knowledge had always been before Him; throughout His life they had laid plans to kill Him.

To a lesser degree, but no less real, are the storms of life aimed at taking us down if we're serving the Lord. The devil hates us and desires to steal from us, to kill and to destroy us. Hell is waiting to devour us. But if, like Jesus, we learn to know our destiny and final destination, then rejoice. Rejoice, knowing that when you're in a storm situation, you're not going to be overcome by it, because God is with you and you are going through.

In the midst of the storm, the disciples feared exceedingly. (Mark 4:41)

What relief they must have felt when they witnessed the Master's power as He spoke and the storm ceased. If you've ever been miraculously healed from a fearsome sickness or disease, you have witnessed God's divine power. Such power brings with it an awesome, glorious joy. And, at the same time, experiencing His mighty power first hand brings us to a reverential fear of the mercies of our wonderful God toward us.

Has God overcome a challenge in your marriage, or

your home, or with your kids? Have you been in an accident and realized that God has preserved and protected you? In times like these we rejoice, and at the same time experience a reverential fear of who God is. Then all you can do is rejoice and thank Him for protecting and delivering you from the stormy circumstance.

No wonder these disciples said one to another, "What or who can this be that even the wind and the sea obey Him?"

Jesus, as always, operated in faith. The disciples were operating in fear. Jesus had stated they were going to the other side. He decreed that in faith and He knew that His words would not return to Him void. (Isaiah 55:11)

What has the Lord spoken to you? Have you heard His voice? Do you take time to think and speak and meditate over what the Lord has said to you? Do you allow the healing winds of the Spirit to flow through you?

Why not, even now, take time to find a quiet spot and speak to God? In your own way, say, "God, I really love You because You love me. I need you. Please speak to me through Your Holy Spirit. Please allow Your Holy Spirit to flow through me, giving me insight and guidance for my situation. Help me to know how to work out the circumstances, the situations, the challenges and problems in my life.

"Lord, please show me how to create the right environment for You to work in my home, my life, my finances, and my health."

As you speak in faith to Him like that, He will help you. He wants to help you to stop the stormy areas of your life.

You have just spoken to God.
Now, speak to the storms of your life.

Remember, speaking to a storm or a situation is the way that faith functions. So, just as Jesus spoke to the storm, you can speak to your own storms – in the authority of Jesus' name.

Speak to any sickness or pain or disease that may have attacked you. Command it, in Jesus' name, to depart from your body, your life, your home. You have the total backing of God's Word to do so. Remind yourself, and your situation that, according to I Peter 2:24, "By Jesus' stripes" you are healed.

And, according to the promise of Matthew 8:17, confess that Jesus bore your sickness and carried your disease, therefore you are healed. Whatever challenges you have in your life, take authority over them, live in peace, and rejoice. Rejoice for you can be certain that what God starts in you, He will complete. He's going to finish fully what He promised. (I Timothy 1:12)

CHAPTER FIVE

Who's Your Faith Buddy?

*"What manner of man is this, that even the wind
and the sea obey him?" (Mark 4:41).*

In addition to being nourished with and speaking out
faith-filled words, it is also crucial to develop the right friend-
ships in life. I call this mutual faith. Having friends in faith es-
tablishes a system of support for those times when pressure
arises in our lives. That's why it's good to have somebody you
can pray with. It's good that you find a friend who will speak
the Word to you and over you. It's good that you have a godly
brother or sister who can encourage you with God's Word
when you're discouraged. It's good that you have spiritual
friendship, fellowship and camaraderie.

When I was a young boy my family lived on a beautiful
lake, called Long Lake. We swam there often as kids. We
weren't allowed to swim alone and were cautioned to always

use "the buddy system." Because everyone does not have equal swimming skills and mistakes or accidents can happen, the buddy system is set up so that every person is responsible to watch out for somebody else. Even when we went to summer camp, the lifeguard would blow his whistle for a "buddy check." Everybody would come out of the water fast and then stand with his or her buddy until the lifeguard made sure everyone was safe and accounted for.

In this life, people who are blown apart by the storms of life usually don't have a "*mutual-faith buddy*." They have no accountability to be answerable to a "buddy check." We all need to hear a lifeguard's whistle. We all need a friend in faith. You need somebody who's not nervous about your challenges and can believe in you like God believes in you. You need somebody who knows that they're redeemed, and part of the Father's family, so they can decree a thing over your life. You need to be nourished with words of faith, both out of your mouth and out of the mouth of a friend in faith. You need to find people who give you the right fellowship and offer spiritual stability.

Being physically strong is very much like being spiritually strong. Both take consistent exercise, which means exercising faithfully. There's even a passage that says, "Exercise yourself in the realm of Godliness." (I Timothy 4:8) You have to exercise yourself "faithfully" over a period of time in order to become strong enough to take on a severe storm. Often when people start a physical exercise program they aren't disciplined enough to follow through on their own. That's why the "buddy check" is so helpful, somebody to be accountable to.

Likewise, you need someone, *a mutual-faith buddy*, to be accountable to when you start a spiritual exercise program. You need someone who will challenge you spiritually where you are lacking. They should ask you if you are living for the Lord. They should ask if you have a devotional life and whether you are giving thanks and glory to God. They should challenge you to see if you are distracted by love for the world and the things that are in the world.

In short, you need a mutual-faith buddy system. You need someone who is a spiritual workout partner, who keeps you accountable, and who helps you grow strong in your faith against the storms of life.

The right fellowship will keep you away from compromise. In fact, the Bible talks about hanging around with people who will let you down. In II Thessalonians 3:14, Paul writes, "If anyone does not obey our word in this epistle, note the person and do not keep company with him." Think about that. We are admonished not to be best friends with people who will take us down spiritually.

Being able to stay strong in a storm is often dependent on whom you hang around with and who you let influence you. If you're going to associate with people who live according to natural things, people who don't understand the concept of calling things that be not as though they are, then you won't be strong in storms. (Romans 4:17) If you give these people too much of your time or attention, or if you give them too much of your trust, they will influence you negatively. They will tear at your support system, tear at the foundation of your life, and bring you to a place where you don't live according to the promises of God's Word. Instead you'll begin living according to the principles of the things you see. (II Corinthians 4:18) You will depart from faith have the wind absolutely knocked out of you.

In speaking to this principle, Paul says, "Those who don't obey the Word in this epistle, note that person and do not keep company with him, that he or she may be ashamed. Yet do not account him or her as an enemy, but admonish him or her as a brother" (II Thessalonians 3:14-15).

From time to time, we may become acquainted with people who don't understand living a life of faith. Paul is not telling us to reject these people, but he is warning us not to make them our closest friends. You must be so grounded in your own faith-walk that with God's Word, you are able to re-sist them as they try to knock the life of God out of you and bring you down into the gutter with them.

Don't allow the devil to use a so-called friend to influence you to flee or depart from the faith. Instead, *embrace* your helper, God's Holy Spirit and His Word and speak out. You can say, "No, wait a minute. I'm going to call things that be not as though they are. I'm the head and not the tail. I'm above and not beneath." (Deuteronomy 28:13)

I am well, I am strong, and I am whole.
God's Word, God's Covenant is working in me.

People who don't understand this declaration think it's strange. They don't understand that what you're doing is positioning yourself spiritually for the storms of life. So, at every pressure point, you are strong and ready for action. You're not going to let your heart be blown apart. You're not going to become a spiritual casualty because of a storm.

God is not against you. He's for you. He really is on your side. That's why Paul encourages us in Ephesians 5:6, saying, "Let no one deceive you with empty words, for because of these things the wrath of God comes upon the sons of disobedience." When you hang around with people who are disobedient to the Word of God, they are undercutting your spiritual stamina. That's why you can't give your heart to ungodly people. They are cynical and don't understand God's Word. It's best that you love them from a distance.

You love these people and you try to speak faith into their lives, but you don't buy into their empty lives. Don't let them take you down for the count. Separate yourself from them. You have to feed on the right nourishment or spiritual food, and then you must find the right fellowship. You need *mutual-faith buddies* to help in life's pressure points.

The Bible is full of pressure point examples. In Matthew, chapter 7, Jesus tells a parable of two guys who heard the same Word, but had very different responses and the resulting end of those actions. One of them did not flee from faith. He obeyed the revealed Word and kept grounded on the rock of revelation. Jesus said this man's life was stable.

But the other guy, who heard the Word didn't obey, didn't *do* the Word. He didn't follow the right procedures and he wasn't nourished in Words of faith. He didn't have the right fellowship. Jesus said this guy's life was pretty shifty and his whole world was built on sand. Sand is a substance that is easily moved. So, when the storm hit this man, his foundation wasn't secure. His whole world crumbled and fell apart.

How strong do you want your life to be? Your spiritual strength and stamina are not determined by somebody else's opinion. Your spiritual strength and stamina are not determined by what you perceive you are able to be or do. Instead, your spiritual strength is totally dependent upon your commitment to God, to knowing His Word, to obeying His Word. It's the whole process of maturing and growing spiritually. God wants us to find the right spiritual nourishment and fellowship to stabilize us.

Find the places where faith is nourished, where the wind of the Holy Spirit can flow. Whether it is a prayer meeting, a Bible study at work, a home fellowship group, a Sunday school class at your church, a mutual faith buddy. Each of these will offer nourishment. Find and commit to as many as you need to become strong in the Lord. If you are strong spiritually, you'll be preserved physically and you will be able to strengthen and stabilize your home, your health, and everything else around you.

Being a storm stopper is determined by how you choose to live your life. In Ephesians 5:1, Paul says, "Be imitators of God as dear children." And He goes on to say, "Walk in love...." In other words, like father, like son. Like Jesus; like you. You and I are heirs of God and joint heirs with Jesus Christ. So, we can have spiritual stamina and strength so we will not be taken down by the storms of life.

Paul then talks about people who really don't want to live for the Lord. "But all fornication and all uncleanness or covetousness, let it not even be named among you, because it's not fitting for saints." Fornication, uncleanness, and covetousness try to filter into your life and take away your spiritual strength. The strategies of hell come to knock you down and to knock you out. When you're down for the count, life becomes so difficult that people let go of faith. They depart from faith and don't even realize they've let go of their solution.

Colossians 2:19 says that all of Jesus' Body is nourished and knit together. All of us receive nourishment and strength from Jesus, the living Word. He makes you strong, not just so you can have victory in your own life, but so you can help strengthen and stabilize others too. Your spiritual stability, stamina, and authority are to be shared, communicated and dispensed. Your spiritual strength is to be exhibited in every area of your life.

In essence, all of us become distribution centers for Heaven. God wants His authority recognized in the earth. He wants His promises to rule over the circumstances that are contrary to the will of the Father. This is why everywhere Jesus went, He used His authority and the promises of God to re-establish God's authority in the lives of people. Whether it was to bring restoration in their body, healing, wholeness, help, or whatever, Jesus' faithfulness became His spiritual stamina in every storm.

This is illustrated well for us in John, chapter 11. Here we read the account of Jesus' friend, Lazarus who had died. Think about that. Lazarus, one of Jesus' good friends, gets deathly sick. Jesus hears the news while He is in another region of the country. The message says, "Come quickly. Lazarus is sick and at the point of death."

But, for reasons of His own, Jesus delayed going there. Many people thought He was too late. But, He is never late. It's just that our timing is not always consistent with what He's doing. When Jesus does arrive in Bethany, He says, "The sickness is not unto death. It is that you would see the glory of God." During a storm, in a pressure point of life, God receives glory when the authority of the Word is pronounced against it and the disastrous storm is stopped.

Storms always cease when God is given control.

The storm faced by Mary and Martha, Lazarus' sisters, was stopped when Jesus arrived on the scene. Lazarus had been dead four days; His body was starting to decay and see corruption. Despite that, Jesus approached the tomb and boldly spoke, "Remove the stone."

People began to freak out. They said, "Hey, Lord, what are you up to? Don't do anything crazy, because by this time he stinks." But Jesus had already confronted the storm and decreed that this sickness was not unto death.

76

When you're under pressure, when everything looks contrary to what you believe, you have to walk by faith and not by sight. Many times in life your circumstances will not line up with the Word of God. That doesn't mean you depart from faith; it doesn't mean flee from faith. It means *stay in faith*, walk *through* the stormy situation with confidence that the Father is leading and guiding you.

Don't give in to circumstances, Speak the Word.

Jesus said, "Hey, remove the stone." Then He spoke to the dead man, "Lazarus, come forth!" Jesus spoke to storms. And now, He's speaking to a dead man. Jesus speaks to demons. He speaks to diseases. *Faith functions with authority when it is spoken,* when it is decreed. Faith always works so don't flee from faith. In Luke, chapter 7, the centurion said, "Speak the Word only and my servant will be healed." Jesus replied, "Wow! You've got great faith." The centurion understood the principle. Under pressure, when his servant was hurt and needed help, he didn't depart from faith.

Don't let the storms of life get you down. Instead, rise up in faith and decree a thing. If you keep feeding on the right food, and find the right fellowship, your faith will be strong. Then, like Jesus, you can decree, "this sickness is not unto death," and say with confidence as Jesus did, "Lazarus, come forth!"

In like manner, you can make a faith declaration to

every situation, whatever it may be. YOUR FAITH can SPEAK to YOUR STORM, and *it will respond!*

CHAPTER SIX

Characteristics of a Storm Stopper

*"Then He arose and rebuked the wind, and said to the sea,
"Peace, be still!" And the wind ceased and there was
a great calm." (Mark 4:39)*

*Things you can do to stay strong
in the storms in your life.*

In previous chapters we've witnessed Jesus manifest
His power in stopping the storms of life – in both His own life
and the lives of His disciples. We have seen Jesus – the Son of
Man – demonstrate His storm-stopping ability.

God not only has a ministry to us, but He wants to manifest through us. God made you to display you. So what the
enemy of your soul wants is to stop God's manifestations in
your midst, in the midst of your storm. But God wants you to
destroy your fear-producing storms, and according to I John

3:8, it's the manifestations of God, the manifestation of the Word that destroy the work of the devil. The Bible says, "For this purpose Jesus was manifested, that He would destroy the work of the devil."

I believe that Jesus' manifestation in your life can stop every storm, stop every pain, and fix every area of your life where you're hurting. God wants to heal you where you hurt. He wants to lift you up where you're let down. He wants to love you and let His love flow through you.

So, examine how you love others. Look at John 13:34-35. Jesus said, "A new commandment I give to you that you love one another, as I have loved you." Jesus is our example of how to love. The way we love our neighbor is the way Jesus did. The way we love our extended family is by following this example of Jesus. He laid down His life. He put what God wanted, what God planned over what His flesh desired. And then He gave this new commandment to us. "By this all will know that you are my disciples if you have love one for another" A faith-filled life is guaranteed when you stay in the love of God.

We have to decide daily to walk in love. The Bible says in Galatians 5:6 that faith works by love. This isn't natural love. It's not constantly having good feelings and some emotional lovey, dovey feelings. This is something supernatural. It is God's love, given and maintained in our lives through His Holy Spirit. The Bible says that the love of God is shed abroad in our hearts by the Holy Ghost. (Romans 5:5)

Jesus' command is very precise. "As the Father has

loved me, I have loved you. Abide in my love" (John 15:9) This abiding takes commitment of time, of communion, of worship, of conversation and of fellowship. But verse 10 of John 15 goes on to say, "If you keep my commandments you will abide in my love." We stay in the love of God when we're faithfully doing His Word. Jesus goes on to say, "Just as I have kept my Father's commandments and abide in His love." He continues, "This is my commandment, that you love one another as I have loved you. Greater love has no one than this than to lay down one's life for his friends."

"You are my friends," Jesus said, "if you do whatever I command you." All of these Words of Jesus are telling you and me as strongly as possible the importance of daily establishing our life in the love of God.

Sometimes the storms in our life are temptations. Temptation is an enticement that comes into our life to draw us away from the love of Jesus. In John chapter 21 we read how Peter denied the Lord three times. Jesus told him pressure was going to come to him. Storms came tempting Peter to deny his association with and his love for Jesus his Messiah. Peter got out of faith and when he heard that rooster crow he wept. He felt so unclean, so dirty because he had abandoned Jesus, and become a faith evacuee.

But, after Jesus' resurrection, He came back and restored Peter. Jesus asked Peter a powerful question, "Do you love me?" Three times Jesus asked him, "Do you love me?" And each time Peter responded, "Yes." Jesus was restoring Peter into His love. Love received is what restores you with faith and function. What a powerful thing is this love that Jesus Is and Gives.

And in John 14:21, Jesus told us how we can know is we are living in His love. He said, "He who has my commandments and keeps them, it is he who loves me." Think about that. Jesus identifies those who are in the love of God as those who actually live and do His Word. This is why the Word of God really has to be your most prized possession. The Word of God is the qualifying ingredient that keeps you in the love of God where Jesus says you can abide. It's not just through emotional goose bumps you feel while you're worshipping. Thank God for our emotions, but the way you really are strengthened in the love of God is knowing and doing His Word.

And as you do His Word, Jesus said that you would be filled with joy. "These things I have spoken to you that My joy may remain in you, and that your joy may be full" (John 15:11). And a life filled with joy overflows in thankfulness.

Being thankful can change the circumstances of your life. Thankfulness grows as we let God's love shine through us. In Romans 1:21 the Apostle Paul writes, "Because although they knew God, they did not glorify Him as God, nor were they thankful." Do you take time to glorify Him? Do you take time to be quiet, and listen to a song, or sing a song, or make up a song, or speak declarations out loud that God is good? It's so important to take time to express our gratitude, and gratefulness, and to glorify Him.

Look what happens if you don't glorify God or thank Him. That same verse goes on speaking to such people saying that you then become futile in your thinking, or in your thoughts, and your foolish hearts become darkened. This is so very important. If you don't take time to glorify Him and thank Him, you will not have the strength to stand in faith in the storms. For God has said that the joy of the Lord is our strength. (Nehemiah 8:10)

That's why you cannot afford the luxury of being ungrateful. There is right thinking and there is wrong thinking. There are a lot of people who love God, but don't know how to think right. Their minds and their thinking haven't been renewed to the will of God. (Romans 12:1,2) Consequently, they live their life letting circumstances tell them what truth is.

Romans 1:22 goes on to say, "Because their foolish hearts were darkened, and they were futile in their thoughts they became fools." Then Paul lists the tragedies, and filth, and garbage that entered into their realm because they wouldn't glorify God or be thankful.

When you have a thankful heart, it keeps your heart tender. People who don't have gratitude, who have become hard hearted, eventually also become hard-headed. Hard-headed people aren't pliable, and flexible, and yielded in their life. They're unpleasant to those around them. Usually such behavior is an indication that they have become hard-hearted. Hard-hearted people aren't thankful people.

The Spirit of God is described as a rain. God wants to tenderize your heart with the rain of the Holy Spirit so you can receive the seeds of God's goodness in your life. It's just like soil that's loosened from the rain so the farmer can plant his crop. The Bible says we should ask for rain in the time of the latter rain. We should ask for the rains of God which are the Presence and the Spirit of God. How do you receive this spiritual rain? You receive it when you decide to be thankful. A thankful heart will keep your heart tender.

When you're thankful, and when you glorify God, you become strong enough to overcome temptation. When you're thankful you can stay in the will of God. That's what the Bible talks about in I Thessalonians 5:18. Paul says, "In everything give thanks for this is the will of God in Christ Jesus concerning you." Being thankful is God's will for you. You don't have to thank God for every circumstance. But you should thank God *in* every circumstance. It says, "*In* everything give thanks," it doesn't say for everything give thanks.

When you are thankful and glorify God you're in a position to be free from futile thinking. You're free from the strategies that the enemy wants to put in your life to bring you down, to make you vile and wicked. Staying thankful keeps you from buying into a bunch of worldly ways that will bring you destruction. So you've got to make a decision that you're going to be thankful.

When you're thankful you receive restoration. Your grateful heart activates the presence and the power of God in a whole new way. Consider the ten lepers who came to Jesus to be healed. After they'd met Jesus and then went their way, they were healed. In other words, they didn't necessarily receive instant healing. But they went in faith with the Word spoken over them. Scripture tells us, "As they went they were healed" (Luke 17:14). As they were going back home in faith, believing that they received what God spoken, then there was a manifestation physically. When the Word is spoken over you, you need to walk in faith with it. As you go through the day, or the next day, God will meet you and validate what was decreed if you continue to believe.

So, as the lepers went on their way, they were healed. There must have been great joy in that group. But only one came back and gave thanks. Only one out of ten, that's 10 percent, responded with a grateful heart. I find that this is rather typical behavior for many people. People cry out for God to meet their needs and God in His goodness grants His promises to them. But then people forget to be thankful in response.

Thankfulness can preserve you and keep you from being destroyed in the storms of life. Let's choose every day to be grateful. Let's tell God thank you. Let's tell people thank you, and let's keep our hearts tender. Let's not be hard-hearted and hard-headed and position ourselves for disaster. Let's not put ourselves in a place where we're going to buy into things of wickedness. Failing to have a thankful heart leads to all kinds of wicked things that are contrary to God.

Verses 24 through 28 of Romans, chapter one, tell us that, "God gave them up to vile passions, even their women exchange the natural use for what is against nature, likewise also the men, leaving the natural use for the woman, burned in their lust for one another. Men with men committing what is shameful, receiving in themselves a penalty of the error which was due, and even as they did not like to retain God in their knowledge, God gave them over to a debased mind, to do things which are not fitting." Today our culture and our world are full of people who have given themselves over to a mindset that accepts such vile behavior. How can anyone accept such things? They can accept such behavior because they don't have a living faith, they don't study and obey God's Words.

If you don't want to end up living such a lifestyle, you have to come to a place where you have gratefulness to God and glorify Him as God. You must continue to be thankful in everything. Keep a grateful heart so you don't lose your tender heartedness. You must take your thoughts captive and keep them pure and grateful to God. And you can do this in Jesus' name. When you do, you position yourself to let the refreshment of the Holy Spirit change you.

To be a storm stopper and not a faith evacuee, follow the example of Jesus. He knew His destination. He had a word. He knew how to overcome low pressure with high pressure. He wasn't a faith evacuee and you don't have to be either. Remember God is Love and that Love is shed abroad in your heart. Put God's Word to work in your life. Don't buy into a way of life that is less than what God has called you to. The Lord loves you, He wants to fill you and free you. He will free you from yourself, and He'll free you from the powers of hell.

Love with a pure heart, keep your faith, refuse to fear, know your destination and remain grateful to Him. Practicing these principles will make you a storm stopper in all the storms of life. You have the living Promise of these things in Christ Jesus. When you experience a storm, know that God's high authority will always nullify any low life pressure that's trying to bring you down. ***In Him, you have become a storm stopper!***

If you would like more information on other materials by
Keith Hershey, please log on www.mutualfaith.org

Mutual Faith Ministries
P.O. Box 951060 Mission Hills, CA 91395-1060